We Knew Mary Baker Eddy

MARY BAKER EDDY
Reproduced from a portrait by Alice Barbour

We Knew
Mary Baker Eddy

The Christian Science Publishing Society
Boston, Massachusetts, U.S.A.

Copyright, 1943, by
THE CHRISTIAN SCIENCE PUBLISHING SOCIETY

All rights reserved

FOREWORD

This volume, published at the request of The Christian Science Board of Directors, contains some addresses delivered at the General Activities Meetings held in The Mother Church Extension on Tuesday evenings following the Annual Meetings from 1937 to 1942. These addresses were delivered by those who had the priceless privilege of acquaintance with Mary Baker Eddy, the Discoverer and Founder of Christian Science, and who shared her warm friendship.

These papers contain many intimate and interesting reminiscences of the type that are universally loved by Christian Scientists, for they tend to keep before the world the uniform kindness, love for humanity, and strength of purpose which characterized our great Leader. They are seven in number and are published as they originally appeared in the Christian Science Sentinel.

CONTENTS

The Discoverer and Founder of Christian Science

ANNIE LOUISE ROBERTSON

IT is a joy as well as a privilege to have the opportunity of speaking about our beloved Leader, Mary Baker Eddy, to a large body of appreciative listeners who also love and revere her.

In "The First Church of Christ, Scientist, and Miscellany" (p. 120), Mrs. Eddy says, "Those who look for me in person, or elsewhere than in my writings, lose me instead of find me." However, it is natural that those who have so marvelously benefited by her writings should love to hear of the human character of our revered Leader; and we who have had the unspeakable privilege of seeing and talking with her, love to recall how uplifting the experiences were, and gladly share them.

It is valuable to have even a slight knowledge of the wonderful way in which the Discoverer and Founder of Christian Science established our Cause on a firm foundation, correcting where correction was needed, and never failing to encourage and inspire the workers, thereby in every way proving her spiritual leadership.

Mrs. Eddy admonishes us in the Christian Science textbook, "Science and Health with Key to the Scriptures," that the "goal is never reached while we hate our neighbor or entertain a false estimate of anyone whom God has appointed to voice His Word" (p. 560). Now if we would share with our Leader the revelation that God gave to her, and which she has imparted so generously to others, it is important that we understand some of the human footsteps which led to the present prosperity and stability of our Cause, and at least catch a glimpse of her true womanhood.

Sometimes a healing has been delayed because of a misunderstanding of our Leader's character; and on the other hand, often a great victory has been won through a sincere appreciation of her service to humanity.

Some of us remember the days when a small congregation, at first less than four hundred people, met each Sunday in what was then called Chickering Hall on Tremont Street, in Boston—an earnest, sincere group striving to re-form their lives into the new way of thinking, living, and healing the sick.

As the congregation at Chickering Hall increased it became necessary to move into a larger hall; but soon this, too, was inadequate to accommodate the ever-increasing congregation. So the students wanted to build a church; but Mrs. Eddy waited until they were prepared to take the responsibility which necessarily would fall upon their shoulders; and under her guidance the original edifice of The Mother Church was built.

As the true idea of Church grew clearer and stronger, the congregation soon more than filled the auditorium; and in 1898, our Leader, awake and alert, gave the order to form branch churches in the vicinity of Boston. Soon, however, still more room was necessary, as the attendance was rapidly increasing; and the students were most eager to build a larger church. Again Mrs. Eddy waited for them to be wise enough to meet and overcome the antagonism which would arise as the prosperity of the Cause became more apparent; and after waiting ten years, she consented to the building of the Extension of The Mother Church. This was a great undertaking, requiring much devotion and sacrifice on the part of the students throughout the Field; and Mrs. Eddy's faith in divine guidance always stood out like a beacon light above the turmoil of mortal existence.

At one time it seemed difficult to find Christian Scientists who were competent to fill the pulpits of the growing churches; and while the church members talked over the matter and worried about it, Mrs. Eddy said little. However, at the right moment she knew just what to do; she appointed two Readers, and instituted the Sunday Lesson-Sermons to become our universal Pastor.

While our Leader always waited patiently for the right time in which to adopt some new and more spiritual method, when it was once decided she brooked no delay; and her living faith always brought its reward.

Christian Scientists owe much gratitude to the little band of workers who loyally and unhesitatingly followed and obeyed our Leader in those early endeavors to prove the teachings of Christ Jesus in healing the sick and destroying sin.

We have a vivid recollection of the joy that came to these earlier workers when for the first time an opportunity was given Christian Scientists to become members of The Mother Church. With what eagerness we sought the way in which we could take this step! This was in Chickering Hall in 1892 and 1893. It seemed to the workers then, as it does now, a wonderful privilege to be able to become a member of the Church of Christ, Scientist.

It was always inspiring to witness the matchless courage and unfailing patience with which Mrs. Eddy guided the formation of the human organization of the Church of Christ, Scientist. It certainly required a strong spiritual conviction to face the opposition of the entire ecclesiastical world, reversing as she did many old methods of ritual service.

As we recall the time when our Leader took an active part in the government of this movement, we do not forget that repeatedly there were errors to be overcome; yet it was a joyous time, for the triumph of truth over error stands out above all as a rainbow above the clouds.

MRS. EDDY IN THE ORIGINAL MOTHER CHURCH

There will be some here who may remember the time, May 26, 1895, when Mrs. Eddy preached in the Original Mother Church. On this occasion she came down from Concord and passed the night in the room which was called "Mother's Room," in the tower of the Original Mother Church edifice. There were only a few church members who knew of her presence in the church—the Directors, the Readers, and two or three others.

Mrs. Eddy did not decide until the very last moment whether or not she should preach. So she requested the Readers to proceed as usual with the Sunday Lesson, and in case she decided to preach she would enter the auditorium and come down to the pulpit. A member of the choir was appointed to watch the door at which she would enter and notify the organist to play, which would signify to the Readers that Mrs. Eddy was coming.

The door did open, and our Leader stood there a moment or two as if in prayer; and then, lifting her head quickly, she walked down the aisle with her usual light, quick step. As soon as she came forward, the organist began to play, the choir rose, and immediately the entire congregation rose. As Mrs. Eddy came down the aisle she turned her gaze toward the congregation, but far above it, as one inspired, apparently unconscious of the audience.

The First Reader came down to meet her at the foot of the steps leading to the platform, and escorted her to a chair that had been provided for her. She sat quietly listening to a solo, and then arose and gave the uplifting address, an extract from which will be found on page 106 of "Miscellaneous Writings." Her voice, without effort, had the most unusual carrying power. This was clearly proved later when she spoke at an Annual Meeting of her church held on June 6, 1899, in Tremont Temple, in Boston.

There were many cases of physical healing in the little church that morning, and many more experienced a change of heart. A friend who had persistently clung to an unreasonable dislike for Mrs. Eddy, told me that as Mrs. Eddy was coming down the aisle she turned and looked into her face, and the resistance melted away completely, her eyes filled with tears, and after that she was absolutely loyal to our Leader. There were many other similar experiences which I heard of at the time.

When Mrs. Eddy was residing in Lynn, also while she lived in Boston, one constantly heard of many cases of healing which she accomplished; and in every one that I heard about the healing was instantaneous. A well-known case was the healing of a man who had been deaf and dumb. For many years afterwards he was at The Mother Church services and often gave testimonies. There is no doubt that much of Mrs. Eddy's healing work has never been recorded.

In speaking of so remarkable a character, of one who had so spiritual a vision, it is impossible to portray it fully. It is simply incomparable—above human praise or criticism, for there are no words that can express what the whole world owes to such a consecrated life.

She was the most consistent follower of the teachings of Christ Jesus that the world has ever known. She, too, reflected the immortal courage that dared to face the whole world and tell it that it was wrong. When Mrs. Eddy talked about the Cause, which she invariably did, it was easy to realize that we were living in a time like that of the early Christians.

Mrs. Eddy had a quiet, most gracious manner, with an entire lack of self-assertiveness that was most unusual. To be in her presence was an inspiration never to be forgotten. In the early days the students loved to speak of her as "Mother."

The Church of Christ, Scientist, is a living memorial to our great Leader and Teacher. Each day it is speaking louder and clearer of the healing message of the Christ, Truth, which she brought to the world.

It would be a great danger to our Cause if Christian Scientists should fail to keep alive the memory of, and gratitude for, the life and sacrifices of our great Leader.

And as we have seen our beloved Leader, Mary Baker Eddy, dedicate her life to the Cause of Christian Science, so now it remains for her followers to consecrate and dedicate their lives to carrying on the great work which she has given into their hands.

Recollections of Mary Baker Eddy

John C. Lathrop

MRS. EDDY writes in "Science and Health with Key to the Scriptures" (p. 25), "The divinity of the Christ was made manifest in the humanity of Jesus," and she also states that "without a correct sense of its highest visible idea, we can never understand the divine Principle" (*ibid.*, p. 560).

During the year 1896 I entered the practice of Christian Science, and shortly afterwards I first met Mrs. Eddy at her home at Pleasant View, Concord, New Hampshire. Her tender, motherly, human reception of a young man, who had just launched out into the deep, and cast his net on the right side of the ship, combined with her remarkable display of intelligence, poise, and love, impressed him deeply with her divine calling and impersonal leadership. After that sweet initiation into Mrs. Eddy's spiritual point of view, the way to me seemed more straight and positive than ever. Two years later I had the great privilege of sitting in Mrs. Eddy's last class, and five years after that of being called by her to join her household at Pleasant View and of witnessing firsthand Mrs. Eddy's human exemplification of Christian Science.

During the eighteen months I was a member of Mrs. Eddy's household, extending over a period of five years, to my knowledge she never remained in bed a single day because of incapacity. As a corresponding secretary I possessed every opportunity of observing our Leader, seeing and talking with her almost daily. Mrs. Eddy's demonstration of energy and activity was highly consistent. Her household was kept continually busy executing the work laid out for them by her.

There is perhaps no better way of indicating our Leader's faith in the healing Word of the Scriptures than was illustrated one night when her need seemed extreme. She turned to her Bible, and, as I have seen her frequently do, opened it at random. Governed by divine intelligence she opened the book to the thirteenth chapter of I Corinthians and read these words: "[Love] . . . beareth all things, believeth all things, hopeth all things, endureth all things." The next morning when she appeared at her desk, bright and well as usual, she told us that, when she read those healing words, she realized that she did not have to bear burdens, that Love bore them all, and she said that then the mesmerism broke and she felt free.

Mrs. Eddy was very methodical, very orderly about everything. She never procrastinated. She never put off till tomorrow the work she could do today. She did it *now*, and expected her followers to do the same. One day she called me to her study and asked me if I was doing my work. I replied, "I am trying to do it, Mother." She repeated her question. I replied as before, and attempted to explain. She said, "Stop, stop!" and gave me one of her penetrating looks which went right through one. "I asked you if you were doing what I gave you to do. You replied, 'I am trying to do it.' Now you are either doing a thing or you are not doing it. Were you doing it?" "No, Mother, I was not doing it," I replied. She said quickly, "When are you going to do it?" "Now," I replied. "Let me see you do it now," she said sternly. I returned to my room. I knew that if I did not do the required mental work now, I would soon be taking a train to my home. The rebuke to mortal mind, to the errors of "self-will, self-justification, and self-love" (Science and Health, p. 242), had been emphatic and merited, and presently a clear spiritual realization was obtained. At that moment my bell rang. Mrs. Eddy wanted me. I went to her calmly and found her smiling, sweet, and pleasant. The error had been destroyed. She did not refer to it again, but gave me more work to do.

One day Mrs. Eddy called the workers to her. Their mental work seemingly had been ineffective and depressing. She said in effect: Never become discouraged, dear ones. This work is not hum-drum, it is growth. It is repeating and defeating, repeating and defeating, repeating and defeating. Is not this the way a mathematician becomes a mathematician? Another time, as I recall, she said,

Humility is the door, honesty the way, and spirituality the summit.

One morning when we were assembled at 8.30 in Mrs. Eddy's study for the usual morning "conversation," one of the household asked her what she thought of the attempt on the part of some Readers in our churches to impersonalize their reading by reading in a monotone. Monotone? she asked. What do you mean? Is it reading such as I once heard when my hymn "Feed My Sheep" was read without expression or emphasis in such a way that I did not recognize it? Is that what you call impersonal reading? Then one said, Won't you read to us your hymn, Mother? At first she hesitated, then smiled, and taking up her book she read aloud to us that wonderful hymn. How I wish the radio had then been discovered, and her reading of this hymn could have gone out to the world! It was beautiful, so full of toneful expression and inflection; and such was her spiritual understanding that we never once thought of her personality; and when she reverently finished with "Shepherd, wash them clean," we felt we had had a baptism in Spirit, and were cleansed of much personal sense, self-consciousness, and fear.

Mrs. Eddy had remarkable eyes, deep and soulful. They seemed to look right through one into the distance, and similarly, when one looked into her keen, deep-set gray eyes, one seemed to look beyond the physical. Mrs. Eddy was light and graceful on her feet, and carried herself with a dignified and queenly bearing. She was outstanding and upstanding, straight and strong, though slight in stature, and about medium height. She was versatile, and always knew just how to approach a person, never forcing the thought with Christian Science, but would present the truth at the right time or not mention it at all.

All are familiar with her balcony picture, which I consider the best picture of her that we have. At the time of the gathering of Christian Scientists at Pleasant View in June, 1903, Mr. Kimball, the Concord photographer, asked to photograph Mrs. Eddy on the balcony. At first she declined, but afterwards said, if he would stand at a distance and not distract the visitors, he might take the photograph. This he did, and that was when the good likeness of our Leader known as the balcony photograph was taken. The small negative was enlarged. Just before the time arrived for her to go out on the balcony to give her address, as a corresponding secretary I entered her room to ask her a question. She invited me to remain in the room and listen to the address through the open window. She then called her maid to put on her wrap and bonnet. It was raining a little, but this ceased when she went out. A multitude of joyous, upturned faces greeted their dear Leader in a stillness indescribable. She started right in and delivered her brief address slowly and distinctly. I was afterwards informed that every word was heard, so clear was her enunciation. She returned to her room and entered, her face radiantly happy. The maid removed her wrap and bonnet and she sat down in her big chair, folded her hands, and said to me, "Wasn't it a wonderful occasion?" Then she asked me, "What are they doing?" I looked below and told her they were having silent prayer. "We will pray, too," she said. "Now what are they doing?" she asked. "They are singing your hymn 'Shepherd,' Mother." After that they repeated "the scientific statement of being" (Science and Health, p. 468). Then they quietly dispersed; and when I told her, she said, "Now I will see what God says about it." She took up her Bible and opened it at random to read the first passage her eyes would light upon. It was Isaiah, thirty-fifth chapter, tenth verse: "And the ransomed of the Lord shall return, and come to Zion with songs and everlasting joy upon their heads: they shall obtain joy and gladness, and sorrow and sighing shall flee away." "See," she said, "how God is always with me. That verse I will add to my address." And this will explain how this Scripture appears at the end of her address (The First Church of Christ, Scientist, and Miscellany, p. 171), when she did not deliver it from the balcony. Then she said, "Now I will take my drive," which she did; and she drove through a big lane of hundreds of her happy followers, most of whom saw her near at hand for the first and only time.

Mrs. Eddy had a very keen wit. She could tell a story or a joke better than anyone I ever knew. I recall an episode, the finish of which was funny. For two years Mrs. Eddy was the honored guest of the City of Concord at its annual autumn State Fair. I remember on one occasion she graciously accepted the yearly invitation and drove around to the Fair grounds at two in the afternoon. She was happily received as she slowly circled the track. She bowed right and left, and seemed to enjoy greatly seeing again her old New Hampshire friends. An interesting incident occurred. Mrs. Eddy asked to witness the exhibition of high diving, and so her carriage drove through to the side of the pool of water where the diver, dressed as Mephistopheles, in red and with tail, was to dive down from a height through a hoop of fire into a small pool of water. Mrs. Eddy had told Judge and Mrs. Hanna, who accompanied her in her carriage, that she looked upon the exhibition as an example of overcoming fear, and she wanted to see it. The moment arrived, and the diver from his lofty height poised and gracefully dived downward through the fiery circle into the water, coming quickly to the surface. He walked out and up to Mrs. Eddy's carriage, bowed low to her and ran off. Mrs. Eddy had invited the First Members of The Mother Church to be present, and most of us were so intent watching her keen interest and pleasure that we missed the actual dive. When the man in red disappeared, Mrs. Eddy turned to Judge and Mrs. Hanna and said, "I beheld Satan as lightning fall from heaven."

The day Mrs. Eddy moved from Pleasant View to Chestnut Hill was beautiful, calm, and glorious. On that day, January 26, 1908, Mrs. Eddy went for her usual drive in Concord. In the meantime her household boarded the train of two cars. All the arrangements were made by Mrs. Eddy. Instead of returning to Pleasant View, she drove to the station and boarded her special car, one of the two. The news spread like wildfire. People scurried. Reporters tried to board the train, but were gently brushed off. Where was Mrs. Eddy going? Was she leaving Concord? were the questions asked. The reporters hastened to telephone to Boston, but just such an emergency had been foreseen by Mrs. Eddy. Arrangements had been made to detour on the Boston and Albany tracks just before reaching Boston. So Mrs. Eddy arrived at the Chestnut Hill Station, instead of at the Boston North Station, thus avoiding many who had congregated at the North Station to see her arrive. At the Chestnut Hill Station, carriages awaited her and her party, and within a few minutes she was in her new quarters in her commodious and beautiful new home. And such was her wisdom never to divulge her plans beforehand, that not a single person, except the few concerned, knew of this momentous move. My mother in New York City had had no inkling of it, and received her first news of the event from the newspapers the following morning.

Mrs. Eddy abhorred all hypocrisy, self-justification, or any excusing of error. She once said she could not teach a person who excused error, who closed his eyes to evil, that that person was not teachable. Someone sent her a set of the three little brass monkeys—"See no evil, hear no evil, speak no evil." That, said Mrs. Eddy in substance, is not Christian Science, it is heathen philosophy. Christian Scientists do not close their eyes to evil, but open them. They open their eyes, spiritual discernment, and awaken to the true nature of evil or sin, to its false claims, methods, subtlety, etc., and then realize its nothingness, its utter powerlessness to control or to harm.

ADDENDUM

The following are sayings of Mrs. Eddy's at various times between 1903 and 1908, which, immediately on returning to my desk, I noted down to the best of my recollection. Other members of the household at the time confirmed these notes as substantially correct.

Every By-Law in the Manual is inspired. I did not write them any more than I wrote Science and Health [showing that both came to her through revelation]. I study Science and Health constantly.

Teach your students, patients, and everyone, to be loyal to the By-Laws, and they will be blessed.

Now measure yourself and your growth by your works, not by your words. All I have ever accomplished has been done by getting Mary out of the way, and letting God be reflected. When I would reach this tone, the sick would be healed without a word.

Don't be satisfied with one victory. Add victory upon victory.

THE PRIMARY CLASS OF 1889
AND OTHER MEMORIES
EMMA EASTON NEWMAN

STILL vivid in memory is the picture of our loved Leader, Mary Baker Eddy, as she addressed the March Primary class of 1889. This class assembled on Monday, February 25, at 10 a.m., at 571 Columbus Avenue, in Boston, in the house which was known as the "Massachusetts Metaphysical College." A limited number might board and room there during class, and my parents and I were happy to be among the number.

The class was held in a large room at the rear of the house. The sixty-five students were representative of our Cause at that time, coming from many parts of the United States and Canada. Some had already been taught by Mrs. Eddy in a Primary class; some had been through a Normal class; some had studied under qualified teachers, and others, like ourselves, had not studied under a teacher.

Our Leader's appearance at that time was of a

woman many years younger than the recorded number. The hair was still dark, the eyes glowing with the inner fire of spiritual inspiration. The delicate complexion permitted her color to vary in response to her thought. The reproduced photograph used in the latest edition of "The Life of Mary Baker Eddy" by Sibyl Wilbur gives a good idea of her appearance at that period.

There could be incisiveness when occasion demanded. One member of the class, a retired minister inclined to controversy, asked Mrs. Eddy how, if people took cold mentally, his little two-year-old child could get cold by walking about with bare feet when too young to be conscious of breaking a so-called material law. Mrs. Eddy vehemently replied, "You took cold for him." She asked one woman what she would do if she were treating a case that did not yield. The answer was, "I would examine my own thought." Mrs. Eddy then asked her what she would do if the case still did not yield. The woman answered she would handle animal magnetism. Again Mrs. Eddy repeated her question, and the woman said, "I suppose I'd give it up." "And that," Mrs. Eddy said, "is just what you should *not* do."

Of course no notes were tolerated, and she questioned each one individually. As a young girl I kept a diary, and on the second day of class is this entry: "Mrs. Eddy is wonderfully clear, and we are enjoying the class beyond anything we ever expected."

Her ready wit was well known to all who enjoyed her friendship or sat under her teaching. She was illustrating the point that "matter and mortal mind are one" (Unity of Good, p. 35), and that mortal mind is the only factor to be considered. She said, "It is like the man who said, 'My wife and I are one—and I am that one!' "

One day after announcing that the subject of that day's teaching would be animal magnetism, she said, "Today we will talk something up to talk it down." It impressed me deeply at the time, and the thought has remained with me that, for lucidity and brevity of statement regarding her teaching of that which claims to be power but in reality is not, these words are unsurpassed: "Today we will talk something up to talk it down."

We all have the benefit of our Leader's own résumé of this class in "Miscellaneous Writings." Here she speaks of the autograph album in which we wrote our names. My father made the presentation, in response to which she said, "Among the gifts of my students, this of yours is one of the most beautiful and the most costly, because you have signed your names" (*ibid.*, p. 281). In emphasizing the necessity for unity among her followers she used solemn words. To quote again from the résumé (*ibid.*, p. 279), she said, "We, to-day, in this classroom, are enough to convert the world if we are of one Mind; for then the whole world will feel the influence of this Mind." In view of present seeming world conditions, how intensified should be our prayer that we, her followers of today, may demonstrate that one Mind. We cannot question that a burdened world awaits our fulfillment of her promise and prophecy. The great and lasting imprint on memory left by our Leader's teaching in the two classes in which I had the privilege to be enrolled, as well as that received in private conversations, is the fact that, while erroneous situations may be considered and discussed, error must never be accepted as real; that error must never have the last word. Always she lifted one's thought to a higher level, and when so lifted she required that there should be no return to the discord.

Her choice of words in which to clothe her ideas in her classroom work was as distinctive and thought-arresting as in her writings. Miss M. Louise Baum, onetime Editor of The Home Forum page of *The Christian Science Monitor*, wrote: "In the writings of Mary Baker Eddy there is this great quality of spontaneous expression. There was somewhat to say that must get said. The freedom and power, the unconventionality and fearless handling of her tool to the end she sought are slowly vindicating themselves in the case of this great writer, and the world is beginning to admit that in the writings of the greatest woman Leader and organizer the world has ever seen is the enduring vitality of great literature. . . . It [her style] is beautiful and strong, and moves with a marvelous celerity to its point; yet it is so weighted with meaning that one may well lift every word as if it were a treasure casket. In this age when a certain smooth propriety of speech is reducing to deadly levels of common-place countless pages of print Mrs. Eddy's writing stands out as individual as the brushwork of some medieval scribe and illuminator of the days before machine-made books. . . . There are no extra words to veil thought or to cover vacancy. She has achieved the great thing: her thinking stands forth in its naked sincerity as if she had done away with the medium of speech and had brought forth the Word itself which is one with thought and deed. . . . She is herself what she says, she has lived it out, and so it is that her words live and kindle life in others." (From *The Christian Science Monitor*, March 3, 1911, International Edition.)

To follow Peter's counsel, "Use hospitality one to another without grudging" (I Peter 4:9), was no task to the mistress of Pleasant View. The cheer, daintiness, and order of the home radiated its owner's individuality. Above all, she gave of herself freely. In June, 1893, during my father's pastorate of The Mother Church, The First Church of Christ, Scientist, in Boston, Massachusetts, we received an invitation written by her own hand, firm and character revealing as were all the letters we received from her. The invitation was to my parents and myself, and we were to arrive in the middle of the afternoon and remain overnight. With what joy we went you can well imagine. We were met at the station and driven to Pleasant View, where Mrs. Eddy received us almost immediately. We were with her practically all the time until eight in the evening, when she excused herself. I was struck by her loving manner towards those who served her. She addressed them usually as "dear," and they addressed her, lovingly, as "Mother." Even in ordinary conversation error was gently rebuked. Someone had spoken of a rather flagrant mistake some Scientist had made. She remarked on how easy it was to uncover *other* people's errors.

She was a remarkably good listener, but above all one realized that she listened to God; that she walked with her hand in God's hand. In a letter dated March 10, 1893, she had written to my father when he began his pastorate: "I found it essential, when the pastor of this church, to lead them by my own state of love and spirituality. By fervor in speaking the Word, by tenderness in searching into their needs—and specially by *feeling myself* and uttering the *spirit* of Christian Science—together with the letter." Her commendation produced the effect of causing one to see one's shortcomings and at the same time determine to overcome them. When she spoke of Christ Jesus, it seemed as if time and space, the barrier of two millenniums and two hemispheres, were swept away. She spoke at this time with ardor of her work on her illustrated poem, "Christ and Christmas." It was evidently dear to her heart. The verse on page 39 of this poem shows our Leader's utter realization that the human self was not a factor in her writing, but, rather, that it was set aside that the revealed

Science of Christianity might freely flow. This stanza reads as follows:

> "As in blest Palestina's hour,
>   So in our age,
>   'Tis the same hand unfolds His power,
>   And writes the page."

The following morning of this visit we were called to breakfast about seven-thirty. Mrs. Eddy greeted us and sat at the head of her table, but she explained that she had breakfasted much earlier and that she would talk while we ate. Again she gave us generously of her time until our departure, about eleven o'clock. It was like class teaching all over again, and impressions deeper than words remained and governed thought. On leaving Pleasant View we drove through Concord and on a few miles to Boscawen to call on my grandfather's cousin, Bartlett Corser. For the first time we heard with great interest from him of his father's and his own intimate friendship with the Baker family, his father being the Rev. Enoch Corser spoken of by our Leader (Retrospection and Introspection, p. 14; Message to

The Mother Church for 1901, p. 32). Cousin Bartlett was about three years older than Mrs. Eddy,
and his memories of her girlhood were beautiful and
distinct. Much of this has been recorded in Sibyl
Wilbur's biography of our Leader (pp. 31–33). On
our return to Boston my mother wrote to Mrs. Eddy
of our deep gratitude for the precious hours spent
with her, and also told of the call on the cousin and
of his treasured memories of her and her home and
family. Immediately a reply, dated July 2, 1893,
was received which contained this paragraph: "Your
letter was an oasis. It was like lying down in green
pastures beside *still* waters. . . . Nothing could have
given me more pleasure, that pertains to earth, than
your account of seeing Mr. Bartlett Corser and of
his relationship! I remember him as an ideal man, a
scholar, a great hearted and great minded man. And
his father, Rev. Enoch Corser, I used to think was
the most *naturally* eloquent gifted preacher I ever
heard speak. It was the sweet memory of girlhood
days that your letter awakened which rested me.
Thank you for it. I shall certainly try to have him

visit me." A few months later Mrs. Eddy wrote a lovely expression of her thanks to my father for a sermon of his which was published in the *Journal* of October, 1893. It read: "God bless you and every day show you a little more of *Infinite Love*. Just your daily bread, more you will not digest."

On the twenty-seventh of December, 1895, came the invitation to New Year's luncheon, with the admonition not to speak to anyone about it until it was consummated—a very usual request from her. We were no sooner ushered into the living room at the left of the entrance hallway than we heard a light, swift step on the stairs, and Mrs. Eddy was taking her guests by the hand and saying, "How good God is to give me this pleasure!" We hardly knew what to say, because we were so conscious of God's goodness to us in permitting us to be there. She explained that she so often had to see people for some specific reason, but that we were "just company."

During the visit she said there were things she wanted to tell her church, and that she should come again soon. The fulfillment of this promise was her delivery of the Communion Address in the same month—January, 1896. (Miscellaneous Writings, p. 120.) In referring to her first time of addressing us in The Mother Church, May 26, 1895, she said, "I discerned every mentality there, but saw no personality." This gave us an enlarged and wonderful sense of what spiritual discernment was, in contrast with the earth-weighted sense of personality. At the table there were five guests, besides the beloved hostess and members of the household. Mrs. Eddy keenly enjoyed a story which illustrated mortal mind's absurdity. Someone told a story of two men in a hotel room. One wanted air and the other did not. Finally, the one wanting air got up, and failing in the dark to open a window broke a pane of glass. Then he could sleep comfortably, but the other man took cold. In the morning it turned out that he had broken a pane of glass in a bookcase!

We were telling her of some of the splendid healings reported at the testimony meetings, and she was listening eagerly, as she always did to any demonstration of the healing power of the Christ, Truth. I said, "Oh, Mother, you should be there to hear them." She smiled so sweetly, and said that she wished that she might. One realized that her retirement from public life in Boston came just at the time the persecutions were lessening, but that had she stayed to enjoy these fruits of her labors she might not have gone on to higher heights of demonstration and worked out the God-ordained plan by which what she called the "stately goings of Christian Science" (Miscellaneous Writings, p. 245) would be forwarded.

On the afternoon of November 19, 1898, I received a telegram reading, "Be at Christian Science Hall at Concord tomorrow afternoon at 4.00" (signed) "M. B. Eddy." In response to similar calls many of us took the train from Boston for Concord that evening. We were all very happy to be called, but distinctly human in our speculation as to the reason for the call. The personnel of this class was much like that of the March class in 1889, except that, indicative of the growth in our movement, there were those from greater distances. England, Scotland, Canada, and our Far West were well represented. Those at greater distances were, of course, notified in time to make the journey. One of the definite memories is the loving way in which she spoke of children. She said that she loved them, that theirs was the white unwritten page, and that it was because of her love for them that they came to greet her as she went on her daily drive. There was the time when she called for a volunteer to read Luke's account of the resurrection. We were all silent until a young man said, "I will, Mother." She said he was her Nathaniel, always ready. She asked us, each one, how we would heal a case of sickness. She listened lovingly and patiently, but she seemed disappointed that more was not said about the healing power of Love, and then she gave us her answer in words which lifted us to a higher vision of what Christian healing really was.

In reviewing the life of the Discoverer and Founder of Christian Science, one sees that dissatisfaction with scholastic theology only drove her closer to God and the revelation of Christ Jesus. Instead of forsaking the Bible, she searched it more diligently, looking for the vital spark which had kept its teachings intact in spite of persecution, skepticism, human philosophies, and counterfeit presentations of Christianity. She lived the Christly teachings in unselfed labors for family and friends, in working for temperance reform, emancipation of the slaves, and higher education for women, until these gleams of light merged into the glory of revealed scientific Christianity. Mary of old said, "Rabboni; which is to say, Master" (John 20:16). Mary of our day said (Retrospection and Introspection, p. 23): "When the door opened, I was waiting and watching; and, lo, the bridegroom came! The character of the Christ was illuminated by the midnight torches of Spirit. My heart knew its Redeemer."

THE WRITINGS OF MARY BAKER EDDY

DAISETTE D. S. MC KENZIE

CHRISTIAN SCIENCE is not something apart from this world, although it is apart from worldliness. It is the way to live. The disciples were not called Christians for many years. The teachings of Jesus were called simply "The Way." This characterization might well be applied to Christian Science in its profound simplicity. It is the way to live. Christian Scientists are not trying to draw converts out of the world to add one more to the sects already in existence. They seek to permeate the human mind with the true way to live, which restores the healing of early Christianity, enriches the affections and intellect, clearing the vision to behold something of the wonders that God hath prepared—wonders which cause us to exclaim, "O world invisible, we see thee." The student learns how his body may become obedient to Mind, how poverty may be banished through balancing his account with God, how he may retain his peace in the midst of discord, how it becomes possible to break the fetters of sickness and sin in the degree of his obedience to God. Is this not truly the way to live?

In a letter written in 1899, our Leader wrote: "All the people need, in order to love and adopt Christian Science, is the true sense of its Founder. In proportion as they have it, will our Cause advance." Some have believed that our Leader had, to some degree, relinquished her leadership of our movement, but instead her leadership rises today more grandly than ever. Christian Scientists are adding to the reverent appellation, "Our Leader," the grander concept of her spiritual leadership of the world. Through the discovery of Christian Science, God is today proclaiming His own government of the universe, and in resistance to this sublime government we hear one human voice after another crying, "No, *I* shall rule the world." This clamor will cease, and out of the fire shall emerge a purified consciousness more ready to learn the way to live. Our Leader encourages us to seek and find her in her writings. The hostility of mortal mind endeavors to separate her from her writings and so keep us from more intimate communion with her. Perhaps we sometimes read Science and Health without a thought of the author. May we not rather realize that we are not only reading the word of God, but that our communion with Him is through the message written by His chosen scribe? Also, in turning our thought to our Leader's other writings, when we seek the teaching contained in her Prose Works, is it not heart-warming to know that she is herself instructing us on practically every subject and situation in life, just as truly as though we sat in her classroom? We may still feel her vital interest in each one of us which we always felt when looking into her face and feeling the warm clasp of her hand.

How shall we attain unto sufficient thankfulness that we have with us these priceless writings, that we are not limited as were the early Christians in the possession of the written word? St. John twice records the lack of more comprehensive writings, implying a regret that all Christians have deeply felt. He says that if the many other things which Jesus did had been written, the world itself could not contain the volumes that should be written. Happily, today all is plainly written for our learning. It must, however, be regretfully acknowledged that there is a world of beauty and wonder in the life of Mary Baker Eddy which is not recorded, and can never be. Even the written word is known to us only in the degree of our spiritual advance. Our teacher has given us ample explanation as to the origin of her writings. She says (The First Church of Christ, Scientist, and Miscellany, p. 115), "I should blush to write of 'Science and Health with Key to the Scriptures' as I have, were it of human origin, and were I, apart from God, its author."

On one occasion, when we were visiting with our Leader, she asked if we had seen a painting which was then in her room in the original Church. It pictures a chair in which she sat when writing our textbook. Several sheets of manuscript were thrown on the floor beside it. "The picture is true to life," said Mrs. Eddy. "When the ideas of Truth poured into my thought, I was so careful not to miss anything, that I let my papers fall to the floor. When the moment of revelation passed, I gathered them up and arranged them." In her Prose Works she relates an interesting fact (Miscellany, p. 114): "I could not write these notes after sunset. All thoughts in the line of Scriptural interpretation would leave me until the rising of the sun. Then the influx of divine interpretation would pour in upon my spiritual sense as gloriously as the sunlight on the material senses. It was not myself, but the divine power of Truth and Love, infinitely above me, which dictated 'Science and Health with Key to the Scriptures.'" The prophecy of the Apocalypse was fulfilled—a woman had brought forth a child who was to rule all nations with a rod of iron, unchanging Principle. From that time on she labored to array the child in fine raiment, to clothe the idea in language befitting its divine origin. In her revisions of Science and Health, Mrs. Eddy studied with the utmost care every word of the text, and in a subsequent conversation she remarked that she often studied for months the origin and meaning of one word and its synonyms, before giving it a permanent place in the textbook, and in one notable instance she prayed and waited on God concerning a single word for three years. In thinking of this we may remind ourselves of the need for quoting her writings with correctness. Literary men and women in many lands have paid tribute to the quality of our Leader's writings.

When traveling in Switzerland many years ago, I met a distinguished clergyman in charge of an American church. In talking with him, I found him very hostile to Christian Science, especially to the work of healing. After some heated remarks on his part, he turned to a building which was being erected across the street from our hotel, and exclaimed: "Do you see those men on top of that fifty-foot wall? If they should fall they would be gone and nothing could be done about it." The next day my family attended the service in the Episcopal church of which he was rector. When he started to read the lesson appointed for that day, we were surprised and deeply interested to find that it was the account of the young man Eutychus, who fell from the third loft and was taken up dead, and who was restored by St. Paul. It seemed to us a message to the preacher from divine Love, for later he changed his view of Christian Science completely. Three years later, in 1893, at the World's Parliament of Religions in Chicago, we again met this clergyman as he came from the crowded hall where he had been listening to a message sent by our Leader. He greeted me cordially and spoke with appreciation of the service he had just attended, adding, "No one is educated today who has not read and pondered the writings of Mary Baker Eddy."

In support of this judgment is the following from a book entitled "A Plea for Christian Science" by an English author, Charles Herman Lea: "It will . . . be generally admitted that the true test of all books is the influence they have upon the lives and conduct of their readers. Judged by this standard, Mrs. Eddy's writings must be given a very high place indeed, for probably no other woman, either of this or of any previous age, has so powerfully influenced the world's thought and the lives of so many of its people."

A further example of the esteem in which her literary work is held, is the quotation from a prominent daily paper referring to the writings of Mary Baker Eddy: "The profound scholarship . . . that had penetrated the depths of the labyrinth of human knowledge may be accorded belated recognition. Men of letters . . . read the book which in the artistry of its proportion, the felicity of its expression, the puissance of its logic, its rare grammatical purity, the splendor of its visions, and the sweetness of its message is, in simple truth, a book of books" (Editorial Comments on the Life and Work of Mary Baker Eddy, p. 42).

Regarding the purpose and spirit of this book, I quote from the same source this deep appreciation (*ibid.*, p. 43): "In the assurance she has brought to doubt, the hope with which she has routed despair, the strength that has been given to weakness, the courage that has supplanted cowardice, the health that has banished wretchedness, the glory of the everlasting day into which she has marshaled the wanderers in night's terror—thus, in the grandeur and the permanence and the mercy of her works, she stands justified."

The other writings of Mary Baker Eddy, which she describes as "indispensable to the . . . student," seem to me to be the records of her own demonstration of Science and Health. They are the breaking of the bread of Life contained in the textbook, and are inspired by the same divine Spirit.

Her conviction of the spiritual origin of the By-Laws in our Church Manual is shown in these words in "Miscellaneous Writings" (p. 148): "They were impelled by a power not one's own."

In regard to our Lesson-Sermon, which is carrying the inspired Word over the entire world, no one doubts the divine appointment of its message. Mrs. Eddy once told us how this appointment came about. "My students were preaching," she said, "and were sending me copies of their sermons. They grew worse and worse. Finally one came which was so great a mixture that if I had not known the fact, I should not have been able to tell whether the writer were a Christian Scientist, a spiritualist or a theosophist. I said to myself, 'Something must be done and at once.' I withdrew from all other work, and in solitude and almost ceaseless prayer I sought and found God's will. At the end of three weeks I received the answer, and it came to me as naturally as dawns the morning light. 'Why, of course, the Bible and Science and Health.' " And now every week it is read to us from the *Christian Science Quarterly* that these sermons are "divinely authorized." That our Leader regarded also *The Christian Science Journal* and other publications as founded by the same divine Spirit, is evidenced in an incident which occurred in 1896. A number of letters from Christian Scientists, and addressed to Mrs. Eddy, were published in the *Journal*. Of this she writes (Miscellaneous Writings, p. 155), "If my own students cannot spare time to write to God,—when they address me I shall be apt to forward their letters to Him as our common Parent, and by way of *The Christian Science Journal.*"

As to the origin of *The Christian Science Monitor*, we may glance at past history. It is known that Mrs. Eddy had long in mind the publishing of a daily newspaper, and that she was waiting upon God to direct her. In 1907 there was launched against her what is known as "The Next Friends' Suit." A leading daily in this country assumed a hostile attitude toward Christian Science and, in company with other enemies of our Cause, entered a suit against her, preferring malicious charges. Neither Mrs. Eddy's years, her womanhood, nor her blameless life deterred these ruthless enemies. It was especially hoped to hale Mrs. Eddy into court, where she could be ill-treated. The proceedings dragged through most of that year. All the charges were completely disproved and the case dismissed. How did the Leader herself look at this extraordinary proceeding? In spite of the malice directed toward her, and the reflection upon her lifework, she passed through this fiery trial, and began at once to plan good in return. And so *The Christian Science Monitor* was born. Like Christianity, it began in the manger of humility, but it was attended by the song of angels, and gifts from the simple-hearted and the wise.

In enumerating the writings of our great Leader, it must not be forgotten that she is the author of that profound work, "Christ and Christmas," and of hymns and poems unspeakably dear to those who study them, which have carried physical healing and spiritual comfort to unnumbered sorrowing ones the world over. The rhythm of Spirit breathes its tender cadence of love through them all, recalling her own words that "Beauty is a thing of life, which dwells forever in the eternal Mind" (Science and Health, p. 247).

While every Christian Scientist has the privilege of distributing these sacred writings, the opportunity of doing so in the appointed order belongs especially to our Reading Rooms and our Distribution Committees. Mrs. Eddy once spoke of "home" as "your calm, sacred retreat." We may think of our Read-

ing Rooms, too, as a spiritual home and sacred retreat for the church members, as well as for inquirers.
In them is spread a banquet of sustaining food for
the seeker after healing of mind and body; the
doubting, the distressed, the bewildered, the weary,
may find in the shelter of the Reading Room the
quiet and peace in which to ponder and pray, and
to gain direction from the intimate Love which is
ever seeking to find that which is lost, to heal that
which is broken, and to comfort "as one whom his
mother comforteth." Our Leader has provided in
the Manual that no reading be done in a Reading
Room except that of her writings, the Bible, and
our authorized publications, and that secular matters
be not discussed, that this atmosphere of calm and
holy meditation may be always found there. May
our church members realize more fully the purpose
of the Reading Rooms, and avail themselves more
often of the tender care shown in providing them.

Our Leader has made it clear throughout her
writings that the purpose of these writings is to
enrich our lives by restoring the lost element of

spiritual healing. Jesus said, "I am come that they might have life, and that they might have it more abundantly," and St. John has added that the written word was given that we might believe, and that, believing, we might have life (John 20:31). Christian Science is the flowering of that believing—believing expanding into spiritual understanding, which the written word has brought us. Let us hold in our forever consciousness that Christian Science is the Comforter promised by the Founder of Christianity, and that it is the complete and final revelation of absolute Principle. It comes to give us "beauty for ashes, the oil of joy for mourning, the garment of praise for the spirit of heaviness" (Isaiah 61:3); to show us the way to live and to live "more abundantly," that we might be called "trees of righteousness, the planting of the Lord, that he might be glorified."

As a parting word, I wish to read a paragraph from a letter written by our loved Leader, which reveals the spiritual animus and purpose of her writings, and of her whole lifework. It was sent to one

Christian Scientist, but is a benediction falling tenderly upon the heart of every one of us: "The Love that looks on this hour must be filling your heart with its Divine Presence, and will hear all your pure prayers to be perfect, and Mother's prayer to keep my child under the shelter of His wings."

Impressions of Our Leader

BLISS KNAPP

JOHN THE BAPTIST was quick to recognize Jesus as the Lamb of God, because John was a spiritual seer. But when the chief priests and elders asked Jesus by what authority he did his mighty works, "Jesus answered . . . The baptism of John, whence was it? from heaven, or of men? And they reasoned with themselves, saying, If we shall say, From heaven; he will say unto us, Why did ye not then believe him? But if we shall say, Of men; we fear the people; for all hold John as a prophet. And they answered Jesus, and said, We cannot tell. And he said unto them, Neither tell I you by what authority I do these things" (Matthew 21:24–27). Jesus knew that spiritual things must be spiritually discerned, and he had the wisdom to let his heaven-bestowed authority remain a mystery to them.

The crucifixion of Jesus caused the world to doubt his teachings. When he came victoriously out of the tomb, he discovered that two of his disciples were questioning his Messiahship while on their way to Emmaus. Seeing the need of defending his ministry, he "drew near, and went with them. . . . And beginning at Moses and all the prophets, he expounded unto them in all the scriptures the things concerning himself" (Luke 24:15, 27). He knew where those prophetic references were in the Old Testament writings, and he explained their application to himself. When the disciples' eyes were opened, and they saw their Master's true identity in Biblical prophecy, that spiritual comprehension of Jesus' place in prophecy closed their minds to any further disloyalty.

Whether we know it or not, we today are being tested in regard to the teachings of Mary Baker Eddy. Are they from heaven, or of men? Those who think of her as just the daughter of Mark Baker might regard her as only another religious leader; but Mrs. Eddy explained her own place in Biblical prophecy, even as Jesus had explained his place in prophecy on the way to Emmaus.

We are familiar with Mrs. Eddy's statement (Miscellany, p. 120), "Those who look for me in person, or elsewhere than in my writings, lose me instead of find me." But she also says (*ibid.*, p. 133), "My book is not all you know of me." And why? Because the remainder of what we can know of her true selfhood must be found in the Bible, in both the Old and the New Testament. That is why the Bible Lesson Committee is never at a loss to find suitable references in the Bible for the lesson on Christian Science. Mrs. Eddy has said (*ibid.*, p. 143), "It is self-evident that the discoverer of an eternal truth cannot be a temporal fraud."

My father and mother were among Mrs. Eddy's early students. When they first took class instruction with her, Mrs. Eddy had not yet included in Science and Health her explanation of the twelfth chapter of the book of Revelation. However, she gave an oral explanation of that chapter to the class. The first verse reads as follows: "And there appeared a great wonder in heaven; a woman clothed with the sun, and the moon under her feet, and upon her head a crown of twelve stars." As my father sat there listening to her explanation of that Scriptural verse, he exclaimed, "Thou art the woman." By this is meant that Mrs. Eddy, in her human experience, represented the woman of the Apocalypse, for as Mrs. Eddy states in Science and Health (p. 565) the Christ-idea was "represented first by man and, according to the Revelator, last by woman."

I shall always remember my first meeting with Mrs. Eddy. It was when she came to spend a few days in our home. I was a very shy lad, especially at the approach of strangers; but Mrs. Eddy's love was so apparent that it melted all my shyness from the first moment that I saw her. We had some baby chicks at the time, and I thought it would interest her to see one, and it did. When I placed that little chicken in her hands, she seemed very much pleased, and talked to me about my pets. This incident must have impressed her in some way, because she remembered it and sometimes told the members of her household about it. She even recalled it to me more than once in later years. From the time of that introduction, Mrs. Eddy gained my absolute confidence and trust. It was just as natural for me to seek her counsel and advice as it was for me to take my problems to my mother, and she invariably gave my questions her loving consideration.

I shall always remember another incident during Mrs. Eddy's visit to our home. She had been awake all night in prayer over some problem, and had not gained her peace with the coming of dawn. Just before breakfast, my sister sat down at the organ and began to play and sing that old gospel hymn, "Joy cometh in the morning." My father, who was a member of the local church choir, joined in the singing, and they sang with such spirit that Mrs. Eddy came out of her room with a radiant face; the song had brought her refreshment and an answer to her prayers. She remembered this incident also, for she wrote to my father, "Sing again the old sacred song referred to on the first page of this letter—and sing it in the spirit you had in N. Hampshire when you sung it *years ago*." Part of that hymn is now included in our Christian Science Hymnal, as hymn number 425.

Calvin Frye once laughingly told me how he tried to dissuade Mrs. Eddy from appointing me to the Board of Lectureship by reminding her of my extreme shyness and inexperience. He even told her she was making a mistake, but she brushed his advice aside and made the appointment. In addition to her prayers for me, she sent me a little book on elocution, and edited my first lecture in her own handwriting. When she returned my lecture, she wrote a comforting and helpful letter which wrought wonders in carrying me through that critical period of learning how to meet public criticism.

One time when my father had to see Mrs. Eddy on some church matters, he took me with him. It was a hot summer's day, and we walked out to Pleasant View. When we arrived, Mrs. Eddy noticed that I was perspiring, and she asked if I would like a fan. Her question embarrassed me somewhat, and I declined with thanks. However, she insisted that I should have a special fan, which she asked Calvin Frye to bring her. While he was getting the fan, Mrs. Eddy told me a most interesting story about it. A former slave in the southland had made it of turkey feathers, and it was presented to Mrs. Eddy by a dear friend in gratitude and remembrance. Evidently the fan meant a great deal to her, for she talked about it so much; and I began to sense that she was trying to teach me some lesson by means of it. When Mr. Frye finally handed me the fan, I began to examine it as an object of interest. Then Mrs. Eddy said, "I want you to use that fan." Obediently, I began to use it in the natural way, and then she took my father into another room for a private conference.

On the way back to the hotel, I began to wonder if there could be any reference to a fan in the Glossary to Science and Health. To my joy, I found the following definition (p. 586): "FAN. Separator of fable from fact; that which gives action to thought." Not fully satisfied, I consulted the Concordance to Science and Health, as soon as I reached home, and found this reference on page 466: "The Science of Christianity comes with fan in hand to separate the chaff from the wheat."

That fan is today in Mrs. Eddy's home at Chestnut Hill, and any visitor to her private room on the second floor may see it. We should remember that John the Baptist came with "fan in hand," and this "separator of fable from fact" enabled him to see Jesus as the Lamb of God.

In these days of world revolution, when there is so much mental confusion, we all need that "separator of fable from fact;" and we shall be most secure if we approach all our problems with "fan in hand."

Some time after that experience with the fan, I began to recall a story which I used to read in school; it was the story of the Key Flower by Bayard Taylor, which is in Swinton's Fourth Reader. I was so impressed by the story that I finally wrote a summary of it to Mrs. Eddy, and drew from it a certain analogy to her. I am sure you will be glad to hear the story and her response to it.

Briefly the story is as follows. One summer's day a shepherd was tending his sheep, when he discovered an unusual flower. As he picked it for closer examination, he noticed a door in the side of the mountain. It was strange that he had never noticed it before; but there it was, and it was open. Cautiously passing along a corridor, he entered a large room filled with chests of gold and diamonds. Then he saw, seated in a chair, an old dwarf with a long beard. The dwarf greeted him kindly and said, "Take what you want, and don't forget the best."

Placing the flower on the table, the shepherd proceeded to fill his pockets and hat with the gold and diamonds. Occasionally the old dwarf would remind him not to forget the best. When the shepherd could carry no more, he turned to leave. On reaching the door, he heard the voice for the last time crying out, "Don't forget the best." The next minute the shepherd was out in the pasture. As he looked around, the door had vanished; his pockets and hat had grown light all at once, and instead of gold and diamonds, he found nothing but dry leaves and pebbles. He was as poor as ever, because he had forgotten the best. The flower which he had left on the table in the dwarf's room was the Key Flower, and had he kept it, the gold and diamonds would have stayed so, and the door of the treasure room would have been open to him whenever he might wish to enter.

I told Mrs. Eddy that she is our Key Flower. She has unlocked the treasures of heaven; and no one knows anything of Christian Science except as it has come through her. If we wish those heavenly treasures to remain real and demonstrable, we must never permit our Leader to be separated in our thought from her teachings.

Her letter in response is in part as follows: "Your story and its semblance are sweeter than birds and blossoms that I long for; and to think that you love God, and love me by way of remembrance and fidelity, fills my lone heart, feeds my hungry sense of nothing, with home and Heaven.

"I wish I could do more for you, but that is

selfish for it would give me much pleasure. Let me wish only that my prayers for you are righteous, then I know the result will rest in sweet hope of your prosperity, growth in grace, and the knowledge of infinite Love, where no arrow wounds the dove, where are no partings, no pain."

Today people are greatly troubled over world conditions. We are taught in Christian Science that such conflicting forces indicate the breaking up of mortal mind's long-cherished beliefs, and we can rejoice at the overturning of error. But Jesus said of such conditions (Matthew 24:12), "Because iniquity shall abound, the love of many shall wax cold." This is a warning not to forget the best. Let us watch and pray that we be not made to forget nor to neglect our Leader—our Key Flower, who has unlocked for us the treasures of heaven. As St. John has said (Revelation 3:11), "Hold that fast which thou hast, that no man take thy crown."

Loved Memories of Mary Baker Eddy

Abigail Dyer Thompson

"THE lives of great men and women are miracles of patience and perseverance. Every luminary in the constellation of human greatness, like the stars, comes out in the darkness to shine with the reflected light of God," writes Mary Baker Eddy in her message on "Fidelity" in "Miscellaneous Writings" (p. 340). Her own life has radiated the greatest spiritual illumination in modern times, and more and more with the passing years do we appreciate the value of her example.

August of 1886 marks an outstanding experience in my childhood memory. My mother had been called to her first class of instruction under Mrs. Eddy, and I accompanied her to Boston. Because we stopped near the college in a private home, I saw our Leader almost daily. I shall never forget the great joy that I experienced when I first met her. On one of my earliest visits to Boston my mother and I attended a Christian Science service in Chickering Hall. To our great happiness the sermon that morning was preached by our beloved Leader, and at its close I had the pleasure of going with my mother to the platform and speaking with Mrs. Eddy. I can close my eyes and see her even now as she stood before that congregation, graceful, earnest, impassioned, with a ring of sincerity in her voice that held her listeners spellbound as long as she continued talking.

No one who has ever seen our Leader could forget her personal charm. In the days when I first knew her there was the vigor and buoyancy of youth in her manner. Her hair was dark brown and her complexion as shell pink and clear as that of a child. Her dark, luminous eyes deepened and shone with such a rapid change of expression that it was difficult to determine their exact color. During a trip to Europe, I wrote to our Leader asking for a photograph that she considered a good likeness, as I wished to have a porcelain portrait painted in Dresden. Three pictures came by return mail. Upon reaching this country, and before returning to my home, I called upon Mrs. Eddy at Pleasant View and showed her the miniature. After studying it for a few moments she remarked, in substance, The eyes are very brown. Then she added, Artists usually want to paint my eyes brown, but no one seems to know their exact color. Walking to the tower window, she said, Come into the light, dear, and see what you think of them. After looking intently for a moment, I exclaimed, Why, they are a deep gray-blue, and I always supposed they were brown. However, I really think that, like the constant change of expression in her face, her eyes at times took on different hues.

It was my blessed privilege to be a member of our Leader's last class. Through the influence of my mother's deep appreciation of Mrs. Eddy as God-inspired in her leadership, I was prepared to follow with absorbing interest every word of her teaching. I can never be grateful enough for having had awakened in me during my childhood years a love and reverence for the Discoverer and Founder of Christian Science that opened my mind to hear and gave me an overwhelming desire to lay hold on the things of Spirit.

As I look back to many inspiring interviews with our beloved Leader, I cherish them as the most exalted moments of my life. She spoke of spiritual things with an intimacy that revealed her vision vividly to one's consciousness, leaving a deep and lasting impression that was not unlike what the disciples must have felt on the mount of transfiguration.

At one time when our Leader was talking with me of the importance of more and better healing work in our movement, she asked if I had been careful to keep a record of my own cases of healing for future reference. I said it had never occurred to me to take any particular note of them. To this Mrs. Eddy replied with earnestness, as near as I can recall her words, You should, dear, be faithful to keep an exact record of your demonstrations, for you never know when they might prove of value to the Cause in meeting attacks on Christian Science. Then she added, sadly, I regret to say that in the rush of a crowded life it is easy to forget even important experiences, and I am sorry that this has been true of much of my best healing work.

Dear, blessed helper of the whole world, little did she realize that at that very moment she was talking to one who owed years of abounding health to the skill of her own healing demonstrations!

On another occasion when I was calling at Pleasant View, I repeated to our Leader a statement that had been made to me by a Christian Science worker who, at the time, was standing in a position of prominence. I could not reconcile the thought to my own understanding of metaphysics, and had determined the next time I saw Mrs. Eddy to ask her if I was right in refusing to accept it. She said, in substance, Your own interpretation is entirely correct, and in this connection I want to impress upon you one fact: no matter how exalted a position a Christian Scientist may occupy in the movement, never accept what he may say as valid unless you can verify the statement in our textbook, "Science and Health with Key to the Scriptures."

When I first knew Mrs. Eddy I was a happy,

friendly child, with just enough shyness to make me a good listener when with older people, and above everything else I loved Christian Science. Intuitively our Leader must have felt this fact, because otherwise, in the stress of her busy life, undoubtedly I should not have received so many evidences of her loving interest.

Her kindnesses were shown in such small ways as this. The first two or three times I came to Boston with my mother, she had her correspondence forwarded to the Massachusetts Metaphysical College and I called there each day for the mail. Frequently Mrs. Eddy would pass through the hall when I was sorting the letters, and invariably she would pause to talk with me for a few moments. At the time of mother's first class, my sister and I were invited to spend a delightful evening with her.

In my frequent visits to Boston I enjoyed many interviews with this great woman, and one time my mother and I were privileged to be her guests overnight at Pleasant View.

I stand before you tonight a living witness who

can bear glad testimony to the healing efficacy of this marvelous woman's realization of Truth. Twice during my childhood I was instantaneously healed through the tender ministrations of our precious Leader from what the physicians would have regarded as hopeless physical conditions. From babyhood I had been an extremely delicate child, with three generations of serious lung trouble as a background on my father's side. On one occasion, previous to going East with my mother, I developed a severe cold which left me with a deep, hollow-sounding cough. As soon as Mrs. Eddy heard the cough she quickly detected the seriousness of the condition and gave me one treatment, which was all I needed to eradicate completely every vestige of the lung difficulty. The rasping cough ceased at once, and not only did this distressing condition yield, but the whole mortal law which lay back of the trouble was broken, and through the years that followed I have rejoiced in complete freedom from any return of this so-called family inheritance.

A year or so later, when we were again in

Boston, I experienced another instantaneous healing as the result of our Leader's powerful realization of Truth. This time I was stricken suddenly and confined to my bed with a most distressing hip trouble. For more than a week, night and day, I lay racked with pain, steadily growing weaker, until the symptoms appeared most alarming. My mother then turned to our Leader for counsel. Mrs. Eddy, knowing that she had been carrying the case alone and at the same time giving me constant nursing care, probably felt that the condition was becoming too real to her thought, and to relieve this situation advised putting another practitioner on the case. The one she suggested worked earnestly for a few days, but the suffering continued unabated.

Finally the pain became so intense that my dear, courageous mother found herself overwhelmed with discouragement and fear as to the outcome, and in this extremity, after a night of almost unbearable suffering, she hastened at five o'clock in the morning to Mrs. Eddy's home. Mr. Frye talked with her in the hall, explaining that it would be impossible to see our Leader until a couple of hours later. However, Mrs. Eddy heard them talking and, recognizing my mother's voice, stepped to the head of the stairs and listened to the conversation. When mother entered my room a few moments later, even before reaching the bedside, she was greeted with the cheery ring of my voice calling to her the welcome message, "Mother, I am better!" And soon we both realized with the greatest joy that I was not only better but completely healed.

Returning to our Leader's home at the appointed hour, my mother bore the joyful news of the sudden change in my condition, to which Mrs. Eddy smilingly replied, in substance: I overheard your conversation this morning and said to myself, It is time for me to step in on this case and save that child. Hurrying to my room, I dropped into a chair and immediately reached out to God for the healing.

So rapid was my recovery that in a few days I was able to make the journey of fifteen hundred miles to our home in the Middle West in perfect comfort. Through the many years that have followed I have rejoiced in abounding health, and from the depths of a grateful heart I give the entire credit for my freedom to the completeness and permanency of our Leader's realization of the healing power of God.

As I think back through the years that I knew Mrs. Eddy, I always feel that the secret of her great achievements could be explained on no other basis than her at-one-ment with God and her boundless spirit of universal love for all mankind. Prior to my taking class instruction with Mrs. Eddy, this was beautifully expressed to me once by our Leader in conversation, in the words she used to describe her healing work, which, as near as I can recall, were as follows: I saw the love of God encircling the universe and man, filling all space, and that divine Love so permeated my own consciousness that I loved with Christlike compassion everything I saw. This realization of divine Love called into expression "the beauty of holiness, the perfection of being" (Science and Health, p. 253), which healed, and regenerated, and saved all who turned to me for help.

The way Mrs. Eddy said the word "Love" made me feel that she must have loved even a blade of grass under her feet. The spiritual healing that Mary Baker Eddy started more than three quarters of a century ago is increasing in its abundance year by year. As the harvest song of gratitude for Christian Science rises throughout the world, her name will be enshrined in the hearts of humanity; therefore it is natural that her followers are eager, in the words of the Scriptures, to "give her of the fruit of her hands; and let her own works praise her in the gates" (Proverbs 31:31).

Mrs. Eddy and the Class of 1898

EMMA C. SHIPMAN

TONIGHT, in thought, will you turn back time, and go to a modest little hall in Concord, New Hampshire, recently provided by Rev. Mary Baker Eddy for Christian Science services.

It is Sunday morning, November 20, 1898. An unusually large number are in the hall for the morning service. About seventy have come from various parts of the world. The First Reader has chosen his Scripture reading from the tenth chapter of Luke, beginning: "The Lord appointed other seventy also. . . . Therefore said he unto them, The harvest truly is great, but the labourers are few: pray ye therefore the Lord of the harvest, that he would send forth labourers into his harvest."

How these words burn in the hearts of many present, for they know that soon they will be commissioned to go forth to labor for the Cause of Christian Science! Doubtless they are praying that they may be worthy of that commission.

After the morning service they return to their hotels or homes, for some reside in Concord, to wait until four o'clock, when they are to meet their teacher, Mrs. Eddy, and have their first lesson.

Promptly, at the appointed hour, those whom our Leader had chosen are in their places. Mr. Edward A. Kimball is on the platform to read a letter from Mrs. Eddy, from which I shall quote: *"Beloved Christian Scientists:—*

"Your prompt presence in Concord at my unexplained call witnesses your fidelity to Christian Science and your spiritual unity with your Leader. . . . This opportunity is designed to impart a fresh impulse to our spiritual attainments, the great need of which I daily discern. I have awaited the right hour, and to be called of God to contribute my part towards this result. . . . What I have to say may not require more than one lesson. This, however, must depend on results. But the lessons will certainly not exceed three in number. . . ." (The First Church of Christ, Scientist, and Miscellany, 243:20–1, 244:10, 24–26.)

After the letter is read, Mrs. Eddy, dignified, beautiful, poised, comes to the platform. The class rises instantly, reverently and silently to greet her. With a cordial smile and a motion of her hand, she bids us be seated. The spirituality which our teacher expresses is so penetrating, so enlightening, that apparently without effort she turns us from her personality to her message.

She reminds us that some in the class she has not met, so she will call their names and ask them to rise, one by one. As we do so, her clear glance seems to read us, and at the same time to reassure us.

Now the lessons begin. Our first subject is God. His nearness and goodness are brought to our attention, until one feels the unspeakable depth of the riches, both of the wisdom and love of God.

Our teacher calls on some of the members of the class to tell what term for God means the most to them. The majority say it is Love. A young woman who has recently lost her mother, says that Father-Mother God means the most to her. Mrs. Eddy's tender, compassionate look as this answer is given, shows that she knows this pupil's need, and the entire class feels the comforting sympathy in her voice as she gives her approval of the answer.

One of the judges in the class declares that Principle means the most to him. We can see, from the merry twinkle in Mrs. Eddy's eye, as she gives her approving recognition of his answer, that her look is almost saying, "That is just what I expected from you."

Two in the class have answered questions in tones that are inaudible. Our teacher says, as I recall: Speak up! When you speak so you cannot be heard, you virtually say, "I have nothing worthy of saying."

In trying to tell of our Leader's instruction, one feels the inadequacy of words to describe a spiritual experience.

When she said, after showing us the need of knowing God more intimately, "Your God is your life," we felt, Here is the work of eternity. Here is our starting point—to begin to know God.

Mrs. Eddy was perfectly natural, she was ever

alert, with a keen sense of wit and humor, and at the same time, her listening attitude to hear what God would give her to say, was apparent.

One felt the great breadth of her nature which enabled her, in such rich amplitude, to meet all the varying needs of her large class.

Mrs. Eddy presented two aspects to her pupils which were so perfectly blended that one gained, in her presence, the feeling of her perfect harmony with Life.

One aspect was her clear and unfailing spiritual sense; her unswerving reliance on God; her consciousness of His ever-presence, and of His nearness, as a friend is near.

The other aspect was her great humanity; her uncommon, common sense, as shown in her practical application of Jesus' teachings to all the little things of everyday living.

This perfect blending of the spiritual and practical gave us an example of what makes a real Christian Scientist. Who but Mrs. Eddy could have written of Jesus, "Through the magnitude of his human life, he demonstrated the divine Life" (Science and Health, p. 54).

She spoke to us with deepest reverence and understanding of Christ Jesus, the Way-shower, and pointed out the vital necessity of following him.

She called to our attention, as she had to earlier classes, the experience of the three disciples on the mount of transfiguration. She quoted Peter's words, "Master, it is good for us to be here: and let us make three tabernacles; one for thee, and one for Moses, and one for Elias" (Mark 9:5). Our teacher said, in substance, that these three tabernacles are to be in our hearts. One for Christ Jesus, to be built by self-consecration on the foundation of victory over sin, sickness, and death. One for Moses, or the law, built by our strict adherence to the Ten Commandments. The third, for Elias, was for prophetic vision, which can be built only as we are motivated by all that is high and holy.

As she talked, her spiritual insight, her oneness with the Father, gave a radiance and richer meaning to statements in her writings already familiar to us.

At times, she illustrated a point in metaphysics with an anecdote or short story. Once, when she had made us all laugh heartily, she said, as I recall: I like to have my students laugh. A good laugh often breaks mesmerism.

She made it clear that one must overcome the instincts of the carnal mind—go down on one's knees, as it were—and struggle with error until the battle with sense and self is fought and the victory won.

Her method in teaching was first to question the pupils. Her clear insight could detect at once whether they answered by merely repeating the words or from an understanding heart. After listening to the answers, she unfolded spiritual truths according to the need.

She told us that the home of the Christian Scientist is in the understanding of God, his affections and interests are there, and his abiding place is there.

When she asked the members of the class for a definition of the Trinity, it was evident that the answers were not perfect. Mrs. Eddy then made a brief explanation, and a few weeks later she sent each member the following:

THE TRINITY

Father, is man's divine Principle, Love.

Son, is God's man—His image, or spiritual idea.

Holy Ghost, is Divine Science, the Messiah or Comforter.

Jesus in the flesh was the prophet or wayshower to Life, Truth, Love, and out of the flesh Jesus was the Christ, the spiritual idea or image and likeness of God.

MARY BAKER EDDY

This was but one instance of her loving care for her pupils.

When she was explaining the necessity of reducing evil, to use her words, "to its proper denominator,—nobody and nothing" (Miscellaneous Writings, p. 108), she put her hands before her, on a level with each other, as if weighing something in each, and she said so earnestly, as I recall her words, Always balance evil in the scale with nothingness. One saw clearly that evil and nothing exactly balance.

Our teacher called for questions from the class, and answered each one with the ease, grace, and certainty of one who had first solved for herself the problems of human experience.

After she had talked about the great need of love in everything we do, a pupil asked, "Do you mean love of person?" Mrs. Eddy replied, in substance, No, I mean love of good. Then she was asked, "How shall we know whether our love is personal or impersonal?" Her reply, in substance, was, When your love requires an object to call it forth, you will know it is personal; when it flows out freely to all, you will know it is impersonal.

A pupil asked: "Why is it that our healing work is not always the same? One day, our cases are healed, and another day, with the same amount of work, a case is not healed." Mrs. Eddy had a pencil in her hand; she balanced it on one finger, and then, tipping it to one side, she said, as I recall, It is because we have too much weight on the side of matter; then, tipping the pencil in the opposite direction, she added that some day we shall have more weight on the side of Spirit; then we shall always heal the sick.

When the lessons were finished, we were fully convinced that Mrs. Eddy had broken the bread of Life with us; that she had given us more in those two lessons than any other teacher on earth could give in any number of lessons.

A member of the class, Judge Septimus J. Hanna, then Editor of the Christian Science periodicals, wrote in *The Christian Science Journal,* of December, 1898, as follows: "Only two lessons! but such lessons! It were futile to attempt a description or review. Only those who have sat under this wondrous teaching can form a conjecture of what these classes were. The Decalogue and Sermon on the Mount were brought before the class, not in epitome, but in marvelous elaboration. The whole Bible, in verity, was held up in vivid review, and its mighty, yet simple and practical, spiritual import, illustrated in language of superb clearness and picturesque beauty,—faultless in symmetry, majestic in the depth of its spiritual significance. To say that this teaching lifted one Heavenward—Godward,—that it sank deep into the consciousness of all present, is only feebly to hint at the actual fact."

The question is often asked, "Why did some in the class receive a C. S. D. degree, while the majority received a C. S. B. degree, and all had a Normal course certificate?" The answer is simple. According to the rules of her College, Mrs. Eddy —with one or two exceptions—gave the C. S. D. degree only to those who had had at least two courses under her instruction. Only about one fourth of the class had previously had her teaching. When Mrs. Eddy was asked why she chose so many young people for the class, she replied, in substance, Because I want my teaching carried on.

Our teacher followed her direction to teachers in Science and Health. I quote, "Do not dismiss students at the close of a class term, feeling that you have no more to do for them" (p. 454). She answered our letters or had her secretary do so. She called us to her home at different times and did all in her power to promote our progress.

Our beloved teacher gave enlightenment to her pupils but not dictation. After she had made clear the Principle and rules of Christian Science and had illustrated their practical value, she left her pupils free to work out their individual problems, guided by our textbook, Science and Health.

May we all carry steadily the torch which Mary Baker Eddy, the Discoverer and Founder of Christian Science, our beloved Leader and teacher, has lighted for us. May it glow ever brighter and brighter, through the generations to come, unto that perfect day when they shall all know God, from the least of them unto the greatest.

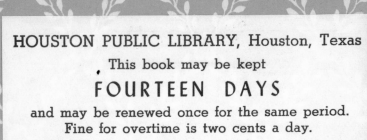